Heidi

JOHANNA SPYRI

Level 2

Retold by John Escott
Series Editors: Andy Hopkins and Jocelyn Potter

Pearson Education Limited
Edinburgh Gate, Harlow,
Essex CM20 2JE, England
and Associated Companies throughout the world.

ISBN: 978-1-4058-4285 3

First published by Penguin Books 2002
This edition published 2008

10

Text copyright © Penguin Books Ltd 2002
This edition copyright © Pearson Education Ltd 2008
Illustrations by Vanessa Julian-Ottie

Typeset by Graphicraft Ltd, Hong Kong
Set in 11/14pt Bembo
Printed in China
SWTC/10

Published by Pearson Education Ltd in association with
Penguin Books Ltd, a Penguin Random House company.

For a complete list of the titles available in the Penguin Readers series please write to your local
Pearson Longman office or to: Penguin Readers Marketing Department, Pearson Education,
Edinburgh Gate, Harlow, Essex CM20 2JE, England.

Contents

Introduction

Miss Rohmer looked at Heidi. 'What is your name, child?' she asked.
'Heidi,' said Heidi.
'That isn't a name for a child!' said Miss Rohmer.

Heidi lives in the mountains of Switzerland, and has no mother or father. Then, one sunny day, she goes to stay with her grandfather. He lives alone in his little wooden house, high up on the mountain. He is an unhappy old man, and hates everybody. But people often change when they meet little Heidi.

She soon has a friend on the mountain – Goat-Peter. And there are Grandfather's two pretty goats, Snowy and Brownie. Heidi loves living with Grandfather on the mountain. Then, one day, her aunt Dete arrives. She takes Heidi to Clara's home in Frankfurt. Clara lives in a fine house in the city, but she cannot walk. Heidi likes her new friend and she learns many new things. But she wants to go back to Grandfather, and to the mountain. What can she do?

Johanna Spyri was born in 1827 in the small village of Hirzel in the Swiss Alps. Her father was the village doctor. After she left school, Johanna studied in Zurich. In 1852 she married Bernhard Spyri and they had one son. Her son died in 1884 when he was only twenty-nine. Her husband died later the same year. Johanna stayed in Zurich and she died there in 1901.

Johanna Spyri wrote many books for children. She wrote *Heidi* in 1880–1881, when she was fifty-three years old. It is her most famous book. You can buy it in forty different languages and there are many films of the story. People of all ages love this story, because a child makes other people happy.

Chapter 1　Alm-Opa

The little village of Dorfli was high up in the Swiss Alps. There were mountains round it – big, beautiful mountains with snow on them. The nearest mountain was the Alm.

High up on the Alm was a little wooden house. An old man lived there, alone with his two goats. People called him Alm-Opa. He never spoke to the people in the village, and they told stories about him. They were not nice stories. When he was a young man, he lost all his father's money. He went away to a different country. What did he do there? Nobody really knew. But in the end he came back – with a son, but no wife.

Everybody liked Tobias, the son. He got work in Dorfli, and then he married a girl from the village. Her name was Adelheid. Soon they had a child, a little girl. They named her Adelheid, too – but they always called her Heidi.

Heidi was only a year old when Tobias died. He was at work in a house when there was an accident. Some wood fell on his head, and killed him. Then Adelheid was ill, and she died soon after her husband. Now Heidi had no mother or father. She did have a grandfather, Alm-Opa – but he didn't want a small child in his home.

Adelheid had a sister, Dete. She lived in a small town near Dorfli. Dete took the child and Heidi lived with her.

But when Heidi was six, Dete met a German woman. The woman wanted Dete to work for her, in her house in Frankfurt. Frankfurt is a big city, and Dete wanted to go there. But what could she do with Heidi?

'I'll take Heidi to her grandfather,' she thought. 'She can stay with him.'

High up on the Alm was a little wooden house.

So one day in June, Dete brought Heidi to Dorfli. She walked quickly through the village. She didn't want to answer a lot of questions.

But a woman saw her and called, 'Dete! Is that your sister's child? Where are you taking her?'

'To Alm-Opa,' said Dete. 'She will have to stay with him now. I've got work in Frankfurt.'

'What!' the woman cried. 'That bad old man? He never speaks to anybody, and he never goes to church. What will he do to the child? You can't leave her with him!'

But Dete didn't stop. They went up the mountain. The sun was hot and Heidi's face was very red. She wore all her clothes – three dresses – at the same time.

After forty minutes they came to a little house on the mountain. There were holes in the door and the roof.

'Is that Grandfather's house?' asked Heidi.

'No, his house is higher up the mountain,' said Dete. 'That's Goat-Peter's house.'

'Who is Goat-Peter?' asked Heidi.

'Oh, he's dead now,' said Dete. 'His wife and her old mother live there. And his son – people call him Goat-Peter too. He takes the goats from the village up the mountain every day.'

They went up the Alm, and they came to a wooden house. It was nicer than Goat-Peter's house. An old man sat on a chair in front of it. He had a long white beard and hard eyes.

'Good morning, Alm-Opa!' Dete said. 'I'm here with Tobias and Adelheid's child.'

'And what do you want me to do with her?' he said.

'The child will have to live with you,' said Dete. 'She can't live with me. I've got a job in Frankfurt now.'

The old man was not happy. 'The child will cry for you,' he said. 'What do I do then?'

'You'll have to find an answer,' said Dete. 'She is your grandchild.'

The old man stood up. He was very angry. 'Leave the child and go!' he cried. 'And don't come here again!'

'Good-bye, Heidi,' said Dete quickly. And she ran down the mountain.

Chapter 2   Grandfather's House

Grandfather sat on the wooden chair. He looked at the ground and didn't speak.

After a minute, Heidi walked round the outside of the house. She found a small wooden goat-house. But there were no goats inside. At the back there were three big, old trees. Heidi heard the wind in them.

'The wind is singing in the trees!' she thought. She stopped and listened.

When she got to the front of the house again, she stood in front of Grandfather.

'What do you want to do?' he said after some minutes.

'I want to see inside the house,' said Heidi.

'Come with me, then,' he said. And he opened the door.

There was only one room in the house. It was a large room. In one corner there was a fireplace. A table and a wooden chair stood near it. Grandfather's bed was in a corner of the room. There was also a big cupboard. In it there were a few clothes, bowls and plates, bread, cheese and meat.

Grandfather put Heidi's things in the cupboard.

Heidi looked round the room. 'Where am I going to sleep, Grandfather?' she asked.

'Where do you want to sleep?' he said.

Heidi saw some stairs in the corner. She climbed up them to a room under the roof. There was hay on the floor. From a window in the roof, Heidi could see the mountains.

'I'm going to sleep here!' she called. 'It's nice here!'

She made a little bed with the hay. Grandfather made a good fire, then he cut some cheese. He put it near the fire, and soon it was brown. Heidi ran to the cupboard. She got out the bread, and two plates and bowls, and put them on the table.

'Good!' said Grandfather. 'I don't have to tell you everything. Now, where are you going to sit?'

He put her on his chair. The table was too high, but the hot cheese and the bread were very good. Then Grandfather put some goats' milk in her bowl.

She drank it quickly. 'That was good milk!' she said.

After they finished eating, Grandfather cleaned the goat house. Then he found some wood and started to make something. Heidi watched him.

'It's a chair for me!' Heidi said after some minutes.

Evening came, and the wind in the trees got stronger.

'It's a nice sound,' thought Heidi, happily

Suddenly she heard feet coming down the mountain. It was the goats. They ran and jumped everywhere. Goat-Peter was with them.

He was a big, strong boy, eleven years old.

The goats arrived at the house, then went down the hill. But two of them left the other goats and ran to Grandfather. One was white and the other was brown.

'Oh, they're very pretty!' said Heidi. 'Are they yours, Grandfather?'

'Yes, yes,' said Grandfather. 'This is Snowy, and that's Brownie. Go and get your bowl, and some bread.'

When she came with her bowl, he took some milk from the white goat. He gave Heidi the milk and she drank it with her bread.

After she finished, Grandfather said, 'Now go to bed.'

'Goodnight, Snowy! Goodnight, Brownie!' called Heidi. The goats followed Grandfather into the goat-house. Heidi watched. Then she went inside and climbed up to her bed in the hay. She was soon asleep.

She got out the bread, and two plates and bowls . . .

Chapter 3   On the Mountain

Next morning, Heidi woke up when she heard Peter and the goats outside. She dressed quickly and ran out. Grandfather was with Snowy and Brownie.

'Do you want to go with them, up the mountain?' he asked Heidi.

'Oh, yes!' she cried.

'All right,' he said. 'Go and wash. The water is outside, near the door.'

He took Peter inside the house and gave him some bread and cheese. 'This is for Heidi,' he said. 'Put it in your bag. And here's her bowl. You can use milk from Snowy for her.'

The two children soon began to climb up the mountain. Peter took the goats to a quiet, sunny place with good grass.

'It's lovely!' said Heidi. The grass was very green and there were mountain flowers everywhere. The sun was warm, but there was snow on the tops of the mountains.

The goats ran everywhere, and Heidi ran with them. They were soon her friends.

Peter pulled the bread and cheese from his bag. Then he took milk from Snowy, and put some of the milk in Heidi's bowl.

'Here's your food!' he called to her. Heidi ran to him.

She ate some bread, and gave some bread to Peter. 'You can have my cheese too,' she said.

'Thank you!' said Peter.

'Do you go out with the goats every day?' asked Heidi.

'Yes,' he said. 'But not in winter – I go to school then.'

'Do you like school?' asked Heidi.

'No! I hate it!' said Peter.

At the end of the afternoon, the sun started to go down. Suddenly, everything began to shine.

Heidi jumped up. 'Peter, Peter! It's a fire!' she said 'The mountains are red! And the sky, and the snow – all red! It's a fire!'

'Peter, Peter! It's a fire!'

Peter smiled. 'It's not really a fire,' he said. 'It always happens when the sun goes down.'

'It's beautiful!' said Heidi. 'Oh, the sun's going now...'

'It will come again tomorrow,' Peter told her. 'But now we have to go home.'

Chapter 4   Grandmother

Every day, Heidi went up the Alm with Peter and the goats. She was soon brown and strong.

Winter was near and the days began to get cold and windy. On very windy days, Heidi stayed at home with Grandfather. She wanted to be with Peter, but there were nice things at home, too. She liked to watch Grandfather at work. Some days he made things from wood. On other days he made cheese from the goats' milk. And Heidi loved to stand under the old trees and listen to the wind.

One night, it snowed. In the morning everything was white and beautiful. But they could not open the door and they had to stay inside the house for nearly a week.

On Sunday Peter came to the house. They sat by the fire and ate meat.

'How is school?' Grandfather asked.

'Bad!' said Peter. 'I can't learn to read. I'll never learn!'

Heidi wanted to know about school, and she asked him a lot of questions. Then Peter said, 'My grandmother wants to meet you. Come one afternoon.'

Heidi wanted to see Peter's grandmother. After two days the snow was hard, and she and Grandfather could go out.

Grandfather sat on his sledge with Heidi in his arms. Then they flew down the mountain to Goat-Peter's house.

'I'll come for you before it gets dark!' Grandfather told Heidi. Then he went up the mountain again.

Heidi opened the door and went into the house. Grandfather's house had one nice big room, but here there were three rooms. They were all small and dark. And everything in them was old.

In one room a woman sat with a coat in her hands. It was Peter's coat. In the corner there was an old woman. Heidi went to her and put out her hand.

'Hello, Grandmother!' she said.

The old woman took her hand slowly. 'Are you Alm-Opa's grandchild?' she said. 'Are you Heidi?'

'Yes,' said Heidi. 'I came down with Grandfather on the sledge.'

'What! Alm-Opa brought you? Did you hear that, Brigitta?' she said to Peter's mother. They were very surprised. 'Tell me about the child,' the old woman said.

'She has Adelheid's pretty face,' Brigitta told her. 'But she has her father's brown eyes.'

Heidi looked round the room. 'Look, Grandmother, there's a hole in the window!' she said.

'I can't see it,' said Grandmother. 'But I can hear the wind! There are a lot of noises in this house when the wind comes. I wake up in the night and I'm afraid. I think the house will fall down on us. It will kill us!'

'But can't you see the window?' said Heidi.

'My child, I can see nothing,' said Grandmother.

'When the sun goes down, the mountains are on fire,' said Heidi. 'Can you see that?'

'No, child, I'll never see the mountains again,' said Grandmother.

Heidi began to cry.

Then Grandmother said, 'Come and talk to me, Heidi! I can't see, but I like to hear you. Tell me, what do you and Alm-Opa do? I knew him well.'

So Heidi told them, and Grandmother and Brigitta were very surprised. 'He's nice to her!' they said.

After some time, Peter came home.

'How was school today, Peter?' asked Grandmother. 'How was your reading?'

'You know I can't read,' said Peter.

'Oh, dear! You're nearly twelve now.' She turned to Heidi. 'Do you see that book up there? There are some beautiful songs in it. I can't remember them now, and I want Peter to read them to me. But he can't learn to read. It's too difficult for him.'

Suddenly Heidi jumped up. 'Oh, it's getting dark! I have to go.'

Outside, Grandfather waited for her. He took her in his arms and carried her up the hill.

That evening Heidi told Grandfather about Goat-Peter's house. 'Everything's old, and the house makes noises in the wind,' she said. 'Grandmother is afraid. She thinks the house will fall down on them. Will you help them, Grandfather? Tomorrow?'

Grandfather didn't speak for a minute. Then he looked at Heidi and said, 'Yes, tomorrow.'

Next day they went down the mountain again. Heidi went into the house to talk to Grandmother. Grandfather stayed outside and worked on the windows and the roof.

Grandmother wanted to thank him, but he stopped her.

'You don't like me,' he said. 'I know that.'

Every fine winter day Heidi went down to see Grandmother. Sometimes Grandfather went too, and worked on the house. There were no noises in the night now.

Chapter 5   Dete Comes Again

A summer and a winter came and went. Now the winter was nearly at an end again.

Heidi never went down to Dorfli. Grandfather went down the mountain sometimes. He sold his cheese, and he bought bread and meat. But he went to a different village.

Two or three times that winter the Dorfli schoolteacher said to Peter, 'Tell Alm-Opa. Heidi has to come to school!'

Peter told Grandfather, but Grandfather did not listen. He did not want to hear.

And then, one day, Dete came up the hill to Grandfather's house. She wore a large hat and a long skirt.

'I've come for Heidi!' she said. 'I know a wonderful place for her. She can stay with some friends of the woman in my house – rich friends. Their daughter can't walk. She sits all day in a wheelchair. A teacher comes to the house and gives her lessons. But she wants a friend. They want a little girl, but not a city child. So I remembered Heidi! It will be wonderful for her!'

Grandfather was angry. 'No, it won't!' he said. 'They'll change her. I don't want her to be a city child. She's happy here in the mountains, with the goats and the birds!'

Now Dete was angry. 'You don't send the child to school,' she said. 'She can't read or write. She's eight years old, and she knows nothing! She's going to Frankfurt! I'm right, and everybody in the village knows that! She's a girl, not a goat!'

'Be quiet!' Grandfather shouted. 'Take her, then! I don't want to see you or your stupid hat again!' And he walked out of the house.

'I'm not going!' cried Heidi.

'Did you hear your grandfather?' said Dete. 'He wants you to come with me. And you'll like it. It's nice in Frankfurt. Now, where are your clothes?'

'Perhaps I *won't* like it,' said Heidi. 'Then can I come and live with Grandfather again?'

'Yes, yes!' said Dete. She took Heidi's clothes from the cupboard. 'Be quick! We have to catch the train from Mayenfeld.'

She pulled Heidi out of the house and down the mountain. When they came to Goat-Peter's house, Heidi said, 'I want to say goodbye to Grandmother!'

'No!' said Dete. 'There isn't time! You can bring her something from Frankfurt. Bring her some nice white bread. She can't eat hard village bread.'

'I know,' said Heidi. 'But look, she's at the window! She's with Brigitta! She's calling to us – what's she saying? I can't hear.'

Dete could hear Grandmother's words: 'Don't take Heidi away, Dete! Don't take her from us!'

Dete did not answer. She pulled Heidi away quickly.

Chapter 6 A New Home

In the house in Frankfurt, Clara Seemann sat in her wheelchair. She sat in her wheelchair every day, all day – and the days were very long. It was evening now.

A big woman in a black dress sat near her. This was Miss Rohmer. Clara's mother was dead, and Miss Rohmer was the housekeeper. Clara's father was away. He was often away.

Clara's face was white and tired. 'When is the Swiss girl coming, Miss Rohmer?' she said. 'Is it soon?'

Then she heard somebody at the door. A few minutes later Sebastian, the manservant, brought Dete and Heidi into Clara's sitting room.

Miss Rohmer looked at Heidi. 'What is your name, child?' she asked.

'Heidi,' said Heidi.

'That isn't a name for a child!' said Miss Rohmer. 'What name did your father and mother give you?'

'I can't remember now,' said Heidi.

Miss Rohmer began to get angry.

Dete said quickly, 'Her name is Adelheid, Miss Rohmer. I'm sorry! This is very strange for her, but she will learn quickly.'

'Well, Adelheid is a better name,' Miss Rohmer said. 'But Dete, the child is very small. Miss Clara is twelve. We want a girl of twelve to play with her. She will have to do the same lessons. How old is this child?'

'I – I think she's ten, or a little older,' said Dete.

'I'm eight now,' said Heidi. 'Grandfather told me.'

'Only eight?' said Miss Rohmer. 'What books do you read for your lessons?'

'I don't have books,' answered Heidi. 'I can't read.'

'Can't read!' cried Miss Rohmer. She turned to Dete. 'Young woman! Why did you bring me this child? How could you make this stupid mistake?'

'Oh, there's no mistake, Miss Rohmer,' Dete said quickly. 'You said, "I don't want a city child." Well, Heidi comes from the mountains. Now, I'm sorry, I really have to go. I'll come and see Heidi again soon.'

And before the other woman could answer, Dete ran out of the house and into the street.

Miss Rohmer did not move for a minute. She was too surprised. Then she called, 'Wait!' and ran after Dete.

Clara looked at Heidi.

'Do you want me to call you Heidi or Adelheid?' she asked.

'My name is Heidi,' said Heidi. 'Everybody calls me Heidi.'

'I'll call you Heidi, then,' said Clara. 'Now you're in Frankfurt. Are you happy?'

'No,' said Heidi. 'But I'll go home tomorrow and take some white bread to Grandmother.'

Clara laughed. 'You're funny!' she said. 'You're going to do lessons with me, but you can't read. What will Mr Kandidat say? He's my teacher. We have lessons from ten o'clock to two o'clock. It's a long time. But he'll teach you to read, and I'll like that.'

'Everybody calls me Heidi.'

Miss Rohmer came into the room again. 'I couldn't catch Dete,' she said, angrily. She looked at Heidi. 'So you'll have to stay.'

It was time for dinner. The manservant, Sebastian, pushed Clara's chair into the dining room. Heidi followed them. The dining room was a large, dark room with a long, wide table.

'Why are there ten chairs round the table?' thought Heidi. 'And why does Sebastian stand behind them? Why doesn't he sit down with us?' Then she saw some beautiful white bread on her plate. She put it in her dress, under the table. 'Grandmother will like that,' she thought happily.

Miss Rohmer didn't see that. 'Listen, Heidi,' she said.

But Heidi was tired after the long journey, and she was soon asleep.

Chapter 7   In Frankfurt

Heidi woke up in a high white bed. Her room was large, and there were chairs and tables and cupboards everywhere. Then she remembered.

'I'm in Frankfurt!' she thought. 'And this is my bedroom!'

She got out of bed. She washed and dressed. Then she went to one of the high windows. She looked out – but she could only see walls and more windows. Where were the ground and the sky?

She went downstairs and found Clara in the big dining room. The two girls ate their breakfast. Then Sebastian pushed Clara in her wheelchair into the sitting room. They waited there for Mr Kandidat. When he came, Miss Rohmer told him about Heidi.

'You can't teach her with Clara,' she said. 'The child can't read!'

Mr Kandidat looked at Heidi. 'We'll start with the ABC.'

Heidi tried very hard. But the ABC was difficult, and she didn't learn anything that morning.

In the afternoon Clara went to bed, and Miss Rohmer went to her room.

'I'll go for a walk,' thought Heidi. 'I want to find some green grass and trees. And I want to see the mountains.'

She went out of the big front door and into the street. She walked to the next street, and the next. There was no grass. There were no trees. And there were no mountains. Then she saw a church at the end of the road.

'I can go up to the top of the church,' she thought. 'It's very high. I can see over the town from there.'

An old man came to the church door. 'What do you want?' he asked.

'I want to go up to the top of the church,' said Heidi. 'Please!'

The old man looked at her for a minute. Then he said, 'All right. I'll take you.'

She followed the old man into the church. They went across to a little door, and the old man opened it.

'Up here,' he said. 'Follow me.'

They climbed hundreds of stairs. When they got to the top, Heidi looked down from a little window.

'Oh!' she cried. 'No grass, no trees, no mountains! Only roofs, and more roofs.'

Sadly, she followed the old man down again. They went past a small room, and Heidi saw a large black cat inside. Next to the cat was a box with six kittens inside it.

'Oh, they're lovely!' said Heidi.

'Do you want them?' the old man asked her. 'You can have them.'

Heidi got excited. 'Can I have them for Clara?' she said. 'She *will* be surprised! But how can I carry them?'

'Where do you live?' the old man asked.

'Mr Seemann's house,' said Heidi. 'Do you know it?'

'Oh, I know every house round here,' said the old man. 'I'll bring them tomorrow.'

'Thank you,' said Heidi.

The old man took her to the church door. Heidi went out into the street again.

'Which is the way to the house?' she thought. 'All the streets are the same.'

She started walking. But it was nearly half an hour before she saw the house. Sebastian opened the door for her and she went in.

Miss Rohmer was very angry. 'Where did you go, Adelheid?' she said. 'Never leave the house alone again. Do you hear me? You bad girl!'

Next morning, Sebastian came into the sitting room with a large box in his hand.

'It's for Miss Clara,' he said. 'Somebody came with it for her.'

He put the box down and went away.

After a few minutes, he heard noises and ran into the room again. His eyes opened wide. 'Kittens!' he cried.

The kittens ran and jumped everywhere. Heidi ran after them. Clara laughed happily, but Miss Rohmer quickly jumped up on to a chair.

'Take them away, Sebastian!' she cried. 'Take them away!' She was afraid of cats. Big cats *and* little cats.

Sebastian caught the kittens and put them in the box again. 'I'll find a nice place for them,' he said quietly to Heidi. Then he took them away.

Chapter 8 Heidi and Clara

The days went slowly for Heidi. Every day was the same. In the morning she went to her lessons, but she did not learn to read. Peter was right. It *was* difficult.

The afternoon was the really bad time. Then Heidi sat alone in her room. She could not go out. So she sat and thought sadly about home and Grandfather.

She was afraid of cats. Big cats and little cats.

In the evenings, Heidi went to the sitting room and talked to Clara. Clara loved to hear Heidi's stories about Grandfather and the house on the Alm. And stories about Snowy and Brownie, and about Peter and his grandmother.

'I've got a grandmother, too,' said Clara 'She comes here sometimes. You'll love Grandmama.'

'Oh, but I have to go home soon!' said Heidi.

She often said this, and it made Clara sad.

'Well, you'll have to ask Father when he comes home,' she said.

One thing made Heidi happy in Frankfurt. Every day she could get more white bread for Grandmother. She always took the bread from her plate at dinner. Then she put it in her cupboard.

One day there was a letter from Paris, from Mr Seemann.

'He's coming home next week!' said Clara. She was very excited.

Miss Rohmer looked at Heidi's dress. It was too small.

'Are all her clothes small?' thought Miss Rohmer. 'I'll look in her cupboard. Perhaps she can wear Clara's old dresses.'

Miss Rohmer went to Heidi's room when Heidi was with Clara. She opened the cupboard.

'Oh!' she cried. 'What – !'

She turned and ran to the sitting room.

'Adelheid!' she cried. 'What do I find in your clothes cupboard? Bread! Bread, in a cupboard for clothes!'

'It's for Peter's grandmother,' said Heidi. 'Please leave it!'

But Miss Rohmer called Sebastian. 'Take the bread out of Adelheid's cupboard and throw it away,' she said.

Heidi started to cry.

'It's all right, Heidi,' said Clara. 'I can give you more bread when you go home. New bread. That bread was old and hard. Now, stop crying.'

Mr Seemann came home the next evening. He came into the sitting room and threw his arms round Clara. Then he turned to Heidi. 'So this is our little Swiss girl!' he said. 'Are you good friends?'

'Clara is always nice to me,' said Heidi.

'And Heidi tells me wonderful stories,' said Clara.

Mr Seeman smiled. 'I'm happy about that,' he said.

He went into the dining room and talked to Miss Rohmer.

'You don't look very happy!' he said. 'Why? Is there a problem with Clara?'

'No, it's the Swiss child, Mr Seemann,' said Miss Rohmer. 'She was a mistake.'

'Why?' asked Mr Seeman. 'What's wrong with her?'

'Everything!' said Miss Rohmer. 'She speaks badly. She brings animals into the house. And she puts bread in her clothes cupboard!'

Mr Seemann went to Clara. He sent Heidi out of the room, and said, 'Now, tell me about Heidi. What are these problems with animals, and bread in the clothes cupboard?'

Clara laughed. She told him about the kittens, and the bread for Peter's grandmother. Then her father laughed with her. 'So you don't want me to send the child away?'

'No, Father!' cried Clara. 'Everything is better with Heidi here! Strange and funny things happen.'

Mr Seemann went to Miss Rohmer again.

'The Swiss child will stay,' he said. 'Be nice to her. My mother is coming soon. She'll help. She likes everybody.'

Chapter 9   Another Grandmother

Mr Seemann stayed for two weeks, and then he went back to Paris. His mother arrived three days later. She had beautiful white hair.

The next afternoon, when Clara was asleep, Grandmama looked for Heidi. But Heidi was not in the sitting room or the dining room.

'Where is the child?' Grandmama asked Miss Rohmer. 'What does she do when Clara is asleep?'

'Nothing!' said Miss Rohmer. 'She sits in her room.'

'Then she's bored,' said Grandmama. 'Bring her to me. I've got some nice books for her.'

'Books?' said Miss Rohmer. 'What can she do with books? She can't read a word.'

'I'm surprised,' said Grandmama. 'Well, she can look at the pictures. Bring her to my room.'

Miss Rohmer left and Grandmama went to her room. Some minutes later, she heard Heidi at her door.

'Come in, Heidi,' she said.

When Heidi came in, Grandmama showed her a big book with beautiful pictures. They were lovely. But then Heidi saw a picture of some young animals on the grass. She started to cry.

Grandmama put an arm round her. 'Don't cry,' she said. 'I understand. You're remembering something about your home. Now tell me about your lessons, child. Are you learning anything?'

'No,' Heidi answered sadly. 'I can't do it.'

'What can't you do, Heidi?' said Grandmama.

'I can't learn to read,' said Heidi. 'It's too difficult.'

'And how do you know that?' said Grandmama.

'Peter told me,' said Heidi. 'And he knows, because he tried for years!'

'Too difficult for Peter, perhaps. But listen, Heidi. You *can* learn to read, when you really try. And when you learn, I'll give you this book!'

'Oh!' cried Heidi, very excited.

In bed that night, Heidi thought, 'Grandmama is very nice,

but I want to go home. And I can't tell anybody because everybody is nice to me here.'

She thought of Grandfather and his little house on the mountain. She thought of Peter, and of Snowy and Brownie. And then she cried quietly.

One day, Grandmama saw Heidi's unhappy face.

'What's wrong, child?' she asked her.

'I can't tell you,' said Heidi.

'Can you tell Clara?' said Grandmama.

'No, I can't tell anybody,' said Heidi.

'You can tell somebody,' said Grandmama slowly. 'You can tell God. Talk to God and ask for his help.'

'Can I tell him everything?' said Heidi.

'Yes, everything,' said Grandmama.

Heidi went to her room. And there, quietly, she talked to God about the sad things in her life.

After that, Heidi talked to God every night.

Two weeks later, Mr Kandidat came to see Mrs Seemann

'I am very suprised!' he said. 'I don't understand it, but –'

'Heidi can read,' said Grandmama. 'Is that right?'

'Yes, that's right!' said Mr Kandidat. 'How did you know?'

Grandmama smiled. 'Many surprising things happen in this life,' she said.

She went to Clara's room. Heidi was there with a book. She read from it, and Clara listened to the story.

At dinner that evening Heidi found a big book on the table by her plate. It was the book with the beautiful pictures.

'Yes, it's yours now,' Grandmama told her.

'For always?' said Heidi. 'Can I take it with me when I go home?'

'Yes, you can take it,' said Grandmama. 'And tomorrow we'll start to read it.'

Chapter 10   Unhappy Days

Every afternoon, when Clara was asleep, Grandmama called Heidi to her room. They talked of many things, and Grandmama listened to Heidi's reading. She got better and better. But Grandmama watched the little girl carefully.

'You're not happy about something,' she said to Heidi. 'Did you tell God about it?'

'Yes,' said Heidi. 'But I don't talk to him now because he doesn't listen.'

'Why do you say that?' asked Grandmama.

'Because I ask him for the same thing every day, and he doesn't do it. How can he listen to me? A lot of people in Frankfurt talk to him!'

Grandmama smiled. 'God can listen to everybody,' she said. 'He hears you. What is best for you? God *does* know, Heidi, and he will help you.'

These words made Heidi a little happier.

But soon Grandmama had to leave Frankfurt and go home. Clara and Heidi were very sad.

Heidi began to read a story to Clara from her new book. This story was about a little girl and her grandmother. In the story, the grandmother died.

'Perhaps Peter's grandmother is dead!' said Heidi. 'I can't go to her now! I can't take her the bread!'

'It's only a story,' Clara told her.

'I know that,' said Heidi. 'But perhaps Grandmother will die before I go home.'

And she cried louder and louder.

Miss Rohmer came into the room. 'Stop that noise, Adelheid!' she said angrily. 'Stop it, or I'll take the book away from you! And you won't get it again!'

Heidi's face went white. She was afraid of Miss Rohmer, and she loved the beautiful book. After that, she never cried again when she read it.

Every night when Heidi went to bed, a picture of the Alm came into her head. There were the snowy mountains and the little wooden house. And Grandfather? Was he all right? Was he dead? She did not sleep for hours, and she often cried quietly.

The weeks came and went. What time of the year was it? Heidi didn't know. She was thin now, and her face was white and tired. She didn't want to eat.

Every night she asked God, 'Please send me home to the Alm.' But nothing happened.

Chapter 11   The Ghost

One morning when Sebastian came down, the big front door was open. 'Who came in?' he thought. He looked in every room, but everything was all right.

The next morning, the door was open again. And it happened the next day, and the next.

Miss Rohmer said, 'Sebastian, you and John will have to stay up tonight and watch.'

The two men waited in a room near the front door. But at twelve o'clock they were asleep.

John woke up suddenly. 'I heard something!' he cried. And he ran out of the room.

Sebastian heard a shout. Then John came into the room again.

'I saw it!' said John. 'A – a white thing, outside! And the door's open again!'

They did not sleep that night.

In the morning, they told Miss Rohmer.

'It's a ghost!' said John. 'There's a ghost in the house!'

Clara heard the story, and she was afraid. Miss Rohmer wrote a letter to Mr Seemann. She asked him to come home. Mr Seemann was very surprised to get the letter, but he quickly came home.

He was not happy about the story of the ghost.

'Somebody's playing games,' he said. 'I'll sit up tonight and catch your ghost!'

He sent for his old friend Dr Classen. Dr Classen was also Clara's doctor. Heidi knew him.

'Is Clara ill?' the doctor asked Mr Seemann when he arrived.

'No, she's asleep in bed,' said Mr Seemann. 'I want you to help me catch a ghost!'

The doctor laughed, but Mr Seemann told him about the open front door and the white thing.

That night, the two men sat in the small room near the front door. They talked for hours. On the table next to them there were two guns.

It was nearly one o'clock when the doctor said suddenly, 'Seemann! Can you hear something?'

They listened.

And somebody opened the front door!

Quickly but quietly, the two men went out of the room. They carried their guns in their hands. The big front door was open. Something white stood outside.

'Who's there?' shouted the doctor.

The white thing turned round with a little cry. It was Heidi, in her white nightdress.

'It's your little Swiss girl!' cried the doctor.

'What are you doing here, child?' asked Mr Seemann. 'Why did you come down here?'

'I – I don't know,' said Heidi.

'She's walking in her sleep!' the doctor said quietly. 'I'll take her to bed.'

It was Heidi, in her white nightdress.

He carried Heidi up to her bedroom and put her on the bed. 'You're all right now,' he said. 'Tell me, child, where did you want to go?'

'I was at home, in Grandfather's house,' said Heidi. 'I could hear the wind in the trees, and I wanted to look at the night sky. So I ran to the door and opened it. I do it every night. But when I wake up, I'm here in Frankfurt.'

'Are you happy here in Frankfurt?' asked the doctor. Heidi didn't answer. 'And where is your grandfather's house?'

'In the mountains,' answered Heidi. 'It's very beautiful, and . . . I want to . . .' She began to cry quietly.

'Go to sleep now, child,' said the doctor. 'Tomorrow, everything will be all right.'

He went downstairs to talk to Mr Seemann.

'The child walks in her sleep because she's unhappy,' he told Mr Seemann. 'She's thin and white and tired. She wants to go home, Seemann.'

'Unhappy!' cried Mr Seemann. 'Thin and white, and in my house! And nobody saw it!'

'Send her home tomorrow,' said the doctor.

'But I can't send her back to her grandfather now,' said Mr Seemann. 'We have to make her well again first, and then send her.'

'No,' said the doctor. 'You can't wait. It's dangerous. Send her tomorrow.'

Chapter 12   The Alm Again

Early the next day Mr Seemann called Miss Rohmer and Sebastian to the dining room. They waited, but he said nothing about ghosts.

'Heidi is going on a journey,' he said. 'Miss Rohmer, please put the child's things into a big box. Then wake her and dress her. Sebastian, go and bring the young woman, Dete.'

Mr Seemann told Clara. Clara was very sad. She didn't want her little friend to go. But her father said, 'Next summer you can go to Switzerland and see Heidi.'

Sebastian arrived with Dete. Mr Seemann told her about Heidi's sleepwalking. 'I want you to take her home to her grandfather today,' he said.

'Oh, I'm sorry!' said Dete quickly. 'I can't do that – we're too busy today. And tomorrow, too.'

Mr Seemann sent Dete away and called Sebastian. 'You will go on the journey with Heidi,' he said. Then he wrote a letter for Heidi's grandfather.

He called Heidi to the dining room. 'You're going home today,' he said.

'Home?' she said. She was very surprised.

'Do you want to go?' said Mr Seemann.

'Oh, yes, I do!' she cried.

Was it really true? She ran up to Clara's room. Clara gave Heidi a bag. Inside was some white bread for Grandmother! Heidi put her big book in the bag, too. Then the girls said goodbye. They could not be sad. There was no time.

Sebastian and Heidi caught the train to Basle. They stayed in a hotel that night. The next day, a train took them to the small town of Mayenfeld.

'We'll walk from here to Dorfli,' Sebastian told Heidi.

Sebastian was afraid of mountains, and he didn't like long walks. He asked a man the way to Dorfli.

'Dorfli?' said the man. 'I'm going there. I can take the child and her box.'

Sebastian was very happy. He gave Heidi the letter for Grandfather, and a small bag. 'This is something from Mr Seemann,' he said. 'Be careful with it.'

Heidi walked to Dorfli with the man. She could see the Alm in front of her now, and she was very excited. When they got to the village, she thanked the man. 'Grandfather will come for the box,' she said.

Heidi climbed up the mountain as quickly as she could. She could only think about one thing: 'Is Grandmother dead?' She arrived at Goat-Peter's house and stopped at the door. She was afraid.

But somebody called from inside: 'That was the sound of Heidi's feet! But Heidi's in the city. Who is it?'

'It *is* Heidi, Grandmother!' shouted Heidi. And she ran inside and threw her arms round the old woman.

Grandmother put her hand on the child's head. 'Yes, it's her hair!' she said, happily. 'Oh, thank God!'

'I've got some nice white bread for you,' said Heidi. And she put the bread into Grandmother's hands.

'Wonderful!' said Grandmother. 'But now I have something better than bread. You, Heidi!'

Heidi told Grandmother about Frankfurt and about Clara. 'But I wasn't happy there,' she said. 'I wanted to come home. And now I have to go to Grandfather's house. I'll come again tomorrow.'

Heidi climbed up the Alm. First she saw the tops of the old trees, then she saw the house. And there was Grandfather, outside on the seat!

'Grandfather! Grandfather! Grandfather!' shouted Heidi.

She ran to him, and they said nothing for some time.

'Did they send you away?' he said, when he could speak.

'Oh, no!' said Heidi. 'They were very good to me. But I wanted to come home to you. Oh, there's this letter for you.' She gave Grandfather the letter, and the little bag from Mr Seemann.

He read the letter, then he looked in the bag. 'It's money – for you,' he said. 'A lot of money.'

They went inside, and Heidi ran round the room and then upstairs.

'Oh! Where's my bed in the hay?' she cried.

'It will soon be there again,' said Grandfather. 'Now, come and have some milk.'

Heidi drank her milk and said, 'Nothing in the world is as good as our milk!'

Soon after that, they heard the sound of many feet. Heidi jumped up and ran out to the goats. Peter stood behind them.

'Good evening, Peter!' she called, and then she talked to the goats.

Peter stood with his mouth open. 'Are you staying here?' he said. 'That's good!' Then he went down the mountain with a very happy face.

Chapter 13　Heidi can Help

Next day Heidi visited Grandmother. 'Did you like the bread?' Heidi asked her.

'It's very good!' said Grandmother. 'Better than our hard black bread. I feel stronger today.'

'The man in Dorfli makes that bread, too,' said Brigitta. 'But it's too expensive for us.'

'But I've got a lot of money!' said Heidi. 'Mr Seemann gave it to me. Peter can buy you white bread every day, Grandmother!'

'No!' said Grandmother. 'I can't take your money.'

Suddenly Heidi saw Grandmother's old songbook. 'I can read now,' she said. 'Can I read you a song?'

'Oh, yes!' said Grandmother. 'Can you really read?'

Heidi read a song about the sun. Grandmother listened, and her face changed. 'Oh, Heidi,' she said. 'That was wonderful. Read it again.'

Now Grandfather was outside, and Heidi had to go. She told Grandfather about her plan for Grandmother.

'But Heidi, you can buy a bed with your money,' he said.

'But I don't want a bed,' said Heidi. 'I want Grandmother to have her bread. Oh, I'm so happy! I can help her because God showed me the way.'

Grandfather looked at her strangely. 'Who told you about God, Heidi?' he asked.

'Clara's Grandmama,' answered Heidi. 'Do you talk to God, Grandfather?'

'Never,' said Grandfather. 'I don't think about God, and God doesn't think about me. I can't go to him again now, not after years and years.'

'Oh, yes, you can!' said Heidi. 'God will always listen to you. Grandmama told me.'

That evening, when Heidi was asleep, Grandfather went outside. He looked up at the night sky and spoke to God.

'I'm sorry,' he said.

The next day was Sunday. When Heidi got up, Grandfather said, 'Put a nice dress on. We're going to the church in Dorfli!'

Heidi was surprised, but she dressed quickly.

There were a lot of people in the church. Heidi and Grandfather found chairs at the back and sat down. But soon everybody in the church saw them.

'Alm-Opa is here!' they said. 'The child did this! It's wonderful!'

Grandfather wanted Heidi to go to school now. But she couldn't go down to the village in the winter. The snow was too thick.

'I'll take a house in Dorfli,' said Grandfather.

He found an old house near the church. At the beginning of the winter they moved there. The next week the snow arrived.

Peter came to Dorfli on his sledge. Every day his mother sent him to school. But very often Peter didn't go. He played in the snow, then visited Heidi.

When the snow was hard, Peter took Heidi to Grandmother.

'Mother's ill,' said Brigitta. 'She's in bed.'

Heidi went to the old woman's bed. 'Are you very ill?' she asked.

'No,' said Grandmother. 'I can eat your nice bread.'

'Your bed is very old,' said Heidi.

'Yes, it's not a good bed,' said Grandmother. Then Heidi read her a song, and the old woman was happy.

The next day, Heidi said to Peter, 'I'm going to teach you to read. Then you can read to Grandmother.'

Peter didn't want to do it, but he came to the house after school every day. They worked with an old reading-book of Clara's.

One evening Peter went home and said, 'I can read! Give me the songbook.'

Every evening he read a song to Grandmother. But it was different from Heidi's reading. He didn't read the hard words!

Chapter 14   Clara Comes

After the winter, Grandfather and Heidi went back to the Alm. In June a letter came from Clara.

'Grandmama and I are coming to Dorfli!' said the letter.

'It's wonderful!' Heidi said to Peter. But Peter wasn't happy. Heidi was his friend. He didn't want her to have other friends.

One morning Heidi looked down the Alm. Two men carried a chair, with a girl in it. Then there was a woman on a horse. Behind her, a man pushed a wheelchair.

Soon they got to the house. Heidi threw her arms round Clara, and the two of them shouted happily. The three men went down the hill again with the horse.

'Oh, I love it here!' Clara said. 'Everything is beautiful. The mountains, the trees, the grass and the flowers.' Alm-Opa put her in her wheelchair, and Heidi pushed it round the house. She wanted her to see the old trees, and to hear the wind.

Then Alm-Opa made the food. They sat outside and ate under the blue sky. Clara finished her hot cheese and asked for more. At home she never wanted more food.

All afternoon the girls sat under the trees and talked. Grandmama and Alm-Opa talked, too. Then Clara wanted to see inside the house, and Alm-Opa carried her in his strong arms. He carried her up to Heidi's bedroom.

'Oh, I want to sleep here!' cried Clara.

'The mountain and the sun will be good for her,' Alm-Opa told Grandmama.

Grandmama looked at Clara's excited face. 'I think it's a very good plan,' she said.

'Now I can meet Peter and the goats!' Clara said.

But when Peter came, he didn't speak to them. He didn't want to meet Heidi's friend.

Clara was very happy. She ate a lot, and she slept well. And soon she began to get stronger. When Alm-Opa carried her down to her chair he said, 'Try to stand.' Clara tried. Her legs hurt, but every day she stood for a little longer.

Heidi wanted to show Clara the place up the mountain.

'I'll push her up in her wheelchair,' said Grandfather.

Later, Peter went past with the goats. Heidi called, 'Peter! Tomorrow we're coming with you!'

Peter said nothing. He hated the girl from Frankfurt. Heidi was always with her, and not with him!

When he arrived at the house next day, everybody was inside. But the wheelchair was outside, ready for Clara. Peter looked at it. Suddenly he was very angry. He pushed the wheelchair down the mountain! It ran down, faster and faster. Peter laughed and ran up the hill.

When Heidi and Grandfather came out, Heidi said, 'Where's the wheelchair? Perhaps the wind sent it down the mountain!'

'Now we can't go up to the high place!' Clara cried.

'I'll carry you up there,' said Grandfather.

When they got to the high place, Peter was very surprised to see them.

'Why didn't you come for Snowy and Brownie?' said Grandfather angrily. 'Did you see the chair?'

'What chair?' said Peter. Grandfather looked at him, and said nothing. He put Clara down. 'I have to look for the wheelchair. I'll come back for you this afternoon.'

Clara sat on the grass and looked at the blue sky and the mountain tops. Then she saw the flowers near her. 'Look at those blue flowers!' she said. 'They're beautiful!'

'There are more flowers there,' said Heidi. She called, 'Peter! Come here!' He didn't move, so she shouted again: 'Come here, or I'll . . .!'

Peter was suddenly afraid. Perhaps Heidi knew about the wheelchair! He came quickly.

'We're going to take Clara to the place with the blue flowers,' said Heidi. 'Clara, put one arm on me, and one round Peter . . . now!' But Heidi was smaller than Peter, and they couldn't carry her.

'Move your foot, Clara,' said Heidi. 'That's right! Now the other foot.'

Clara moved slowly. 'I can do it, Heidi! I'm walking!'

Chapter 15   Surprises

Later, when Peter took the goats down to Dorfli, he saw a lot of people. They were at the bottom of the hill with the wheelchair.

'Wheelchairs cost a lot of money,' somebody said. 'Perhaps the man from Frankfurt will send a policeman.'

Peter ran away. His face was white, and he was afraid.

'I can do it, Heidi! I'm walking!'

Clara walked more and more every day. She wrote a letter to Grandmama and asked her to come again. She didn't tell her about the walking. An answer came from Grandmama, and Peter came with the letter. He pushed it into Alm-Opa's hand and ran away.

'Peter is strange now,' said Heidi.

'Yes, he is,' said Alm-Opa, slowly.

When Grandmama came up the hill on her horse, Alm-Opa, Heidi and Clara were outside. Clara sat on a chair.

'Clara!' cried Grandmama. 'You're not in your wheelchair! And you're not thin and white!'

Clara stood up, and began to walk slowly to her.

Grandmama's eyes opened wide. 'Wonderful!' she said. Then she turned to Alm-Opa. 'Thank you,' she said. 'I have to tell my son! He's in Paris, but I'll write to him.'

'I'll call Peter,' said Alm-Opa. 'He can take your letter to Dorfli.'

But Mr Seemann wasn't in Paris. He was in Dorfli!

'Clara will be surprised,' he thought. He climbed up the Alm from Dorfli. Then he saw a boy. 'Boy! Is this the way to Heidi's house?' he asked.

But the boy ran away. It was Peter.

'It's the policeman from Frankfurt!' thought Peter.

Suddenly, he fell over and went down the mountain. He wasn't hurt, but Grandmama's letter fell out of his hand.

He went slowly up the hill again.

At Alm-Opa's house the strange man was with Clara. Peter tried to run past, but Alm-Opa called, 'Come here, Peter!' Everybody looked at him.

'It – it wasn't the wind!' he said suddenly. 'It was me!'

'What does he mean?' said Mr Seemann.

'He pushed Clara's wheelchair down the mountain,' said Alm-Opa, quietly.

Nobody spoke for a minute. Then Mr Seemann said, 'Then we have to thank him because he helped Clara.'

Peter was very surprised. The man wasn't angry with him! *Was* he a policeman?

Mr Seemann turned to Alm-Opa. 'How can I thank you? What can I give you, my friend?'

'I don't want anything,' said Alm-Opa. 'But when I die, Heidi will have nobody. Can you give her a home?'

'But of course!' said Mr Seemann. 'Now, Heidi, what do *you* want?'

'A bed for Peter's grandmother!' said Heidi quickly.

'We'll send her a fine bed,' said Grandmama. 'And good food, and clothes for the winter.'

'This is a wonderful day!' cried Heidi.

'Yes,' said Mr Seemann. He looked at Clara. 'A wonderful day!'

ACTIVITIES

Chapters 1–3

Before you read

1 Look at the front of this book, and then read the Introduction. Where are the mountains in this story? What do you know about Heidi?

2 Look at the Word List at the back of the book. Then look at the pictures in the book. In which pictures can you see:

a   a beard?   e   grass?

b   bowls?   f   kittens?

c   cheese?   g   a roof?

d   a goat?   h   a wheelchair?

While you read

3 Which is the right word?

a   Tobias was Heidi's *father/uncle*.

b   Dete is Heidi's *mother/aunt*.

c   Heidi's grandfather is *friendly/unfriendly* to the people in the village.

d   Goat-Peter lives with his mother and *grandfather/grandmother*.

e   Grandfather is angry with *Dete/Heidi*.

f   Grandfather makes Heidi a *bed/chair*.

g   Snowy and Brownie are *Grandfather's/Peter's* goats.

h   Peter *loves/hates* school.

After you read

4 Answer these questions.

a   What happened to Heidi's parents?

b   Why does Dete take Heidi to Grandfather's house?

c   Where does Grandfather never go?

d   How many rooms are there in Grandfather's house?

e   What does Peter do every day in the summer?

f   What does he do in the winter?

5 Work with another student. Have this conversation.

> *Student A:* You are Dete. You can't take Heidi with you to Frankfurt. Tell Grandfather why.
>
> *Student B:* You are Grandfather. You don't want Heidi to live with you. Tell Dete why.

Chapters 4–6

Before you read

6 Discuss these questions.

  a Will Heidi enjoy her life with Grandfather? Why (not)? What problems will she have?

  b Will Grandfather be happy with Heidi? Why (not)?

While you read

7 What happens first? Number these sentences, 1–7.

  a Heidi goes to Frankfurt. .....

  b Heidi meets Clara. .....

  c Dete comes back. .....

  d Heidi meets Peter's grandmother. .....

  e Grandfather works on a roof. .....

  f The schoolteacher talks to Peter about Heidi. .....

  g Heidi goes on a sledge. .....

After you read

8 Why:

  a do Heidi and Grandfather stay inside for nearly a week?

  b does Heidi cry at Peter's house?

  c are Grandmother and Brigitta very surprised?

  d doesn't Peter read to his grandmother?

  e does Peter's grandmother want to thank Grandfather?

  f is Dete angry with Grandfather?

  g does Miss Rohmer run after Dete?

  h does Heidi put bread in her dress?

9 Who says these words? Who or what are they talking about?

    a 'She has her father's brown eyes.'

    b 'Will you help them?'

    c 'She wants a friend.'

    d 'Don't take her from us.'

    e 'How could you make this stupid mistake?'

    f 'He'll teach you to read.'

Chapters 7–9

Before you read

10 Will Heidi be happy in Frankfurt? Why (not)? What do you think?

While you read

11 Are these sentences right (✓) or wrong (✗)?

    a Heidi feels sad at the top of the church. .....

    b Heidi buys some kittens for Clara. .....

    c Clara's father works in Paris. .....

    d Miss Rohmer wants Heidi to leave. .....

    e Clara's grandmother teaches Heidi to read. .....

    f Clara gives Heidi a book. .....

After you read

12 Use the best question-word for these questions, and then answer them.

    What   Who   Why

    a .... does Heidi want to see from the top of the church?

    b .... does Miss Rohmer jump onto a chair?

    c .... does Miss Rohmer find in Heidi's cupboard?

    d .... sleeps in the afternoon?

    e .... has beautiful white hair?

    f .... can't Heidi tell anyone about her problems?

    g .... talks to Heidi about God?

    h .... is Mr Kandidat very surprised?

13 Talk to another student. Does Heidi like these things? Why (not)? the ABC   the streets of Frankfurt   the kittens   the afternoons white bread   the big picture book

Chapters 10–12

Before you read

14 When Heidi talks to God, what does she ask Him? Why? What do you think?

While you read

15 Finish these sentences. Write one word.

    a Every afternoon Heidi reads to ....

    b She thinks that .... will die.

    c She is afraid of ....

    d She .... eat much.

    e She .... in her sleep.

    f The doctor says that she has to go ....

    g .... goes with her to Mayenfeld.

    h She gives Grandmother some ....

    i Mr Seemann sends .... for Heidi.

    j Peter is very .... when he sees her.

After you read

16 Are these people happy or unhappy at the end of Chapter 12? Why?

    a Miss Rohmer   **c** Sebastian

    b Clara   **d** Peter's grandmother

Chapters 13–15

Before you read

17 Life is going to change for Heidi, Grandfather, Peter, his grandmother and Clara. How? Talk about it with another student. Then talk to a different student. Have you got the same ideas?

While you read

18 One word in each sentence is wrong. Write the right word.

    a Heidi wants Grandmama to have brown bread every day.   ....

    b Grandfather says sorry to Heidi.   ....

    c Peter learns to sing.   ....

d Dete comes to Dorfli. ....

e Clara learns to read. ....

f Grandmama and Sebastian visit the Alm. ....

g Peter thinks that Clara's father is a teacher. ....

h Heidi wants a new chair for Grandmama. ....

After you read

19 Answer these questions.

    a Why is Heidi surprised one Sunday morning?

    b Where does Grandfather move for the winter? Why?

    c What bad thing does Peter do? Why?

    d How does Clara change when she is with Heidi?

    e Why does Clara's father thank Peter?

20 Work with another student. Have this conversation.

    Student A: You are Heidi. Ask Peter why he is acting strangely. Ask him about Clara's wheelchair.

    Student B: Answer Heidi's questions. Don't tell her about the wheelchair.

Writing

21 You are Clara. It is the week after Heidi arrives in Frankfurt. Write a letter to a friend. Tell her about Heidi.

22 You are Heidi, and you can write now. Write a letter to your Grandfather about your life in Frankfurt. Tell him about the good things and the bad things.

23 How does Dete feel about everything? Was she right when she took Heidi to Grandfather's house? Was she right when she took Heidi away again? Write a conversation between Dete and a friend after the story ends.

24 Grandmother has died. How will people remember her? Write the story for Dorfli's newspaper.

25 You are Heidi. It is two years after the end of the story. What are you doing? Are you living with Grandfather? Write to Clara and tell her.

26 Did you enjoy *Heidi*? Write about the story. What did you like? What did you not like?

27 Heidi changes people's lives when she meets them. Did anybody change your life? Write about that person.

28 You went on holiday to Dorfli for two weeks last summer. Write about your holiday for a student magazine. What did you do there? Would you like to go there again? Why (not)?